Copyright 2022 - All rights reserved.

You may not reproduce, duplicate or send the contents of this book without direct written permission from the author. You cannot apply hereby despite any circumstance blame the publisher or hold him or her to legal responsibility for any reparation, compensations, or monetary forfeiture owing to the information included herein, either in a direct or an indirect way.

Legal Notice: This book has copyright protection. You can use the book for personal purposes. You should not sell, use, alter, distribute, quote, take excerpts, or paraphrase in part or whole the material contained in this book without obtaining the permission of the author first.

Disclaimer Notice: You must take note that the information in this document is for casual reading and entertainment purposes only. We have made every attempt to provide accurate, up-to-date, and reliable information. We do not express or imply guarantees of any kind. The persons who read admit that the writer is not occupied in giving legal, financial, medical, or other advice. We put this book content by sourcing various places.

Please consult a licensed professional before you try any techniques shown in this book. By going through this document, the book lover comes to an an agreement that under no situation is the author accountable for any forfeiture, direct or indirect, which they may incur because of the use of material contained in this document, including, but not limited to, — errors, omissions, or inaccuracies.

GARDEN PLANNER JOURNAL

Monthly Garden Calendar
Month:_____

SUN	MON	TUE	WED	THU	FRD	SAT
☐	☐	☐	☐	☐	☐	☐
☐	☐	☐	☐	☐	☐	☐
☐	☐	☐	☐	☐	☐	☐
☐	☐	☐	☐	☐	☐	☐
☐	☐	☐	☐	☐	☐	☐
☐	☐	☐	☐	☐	☐	☐

Notes

Garden Layout

Garden Layout

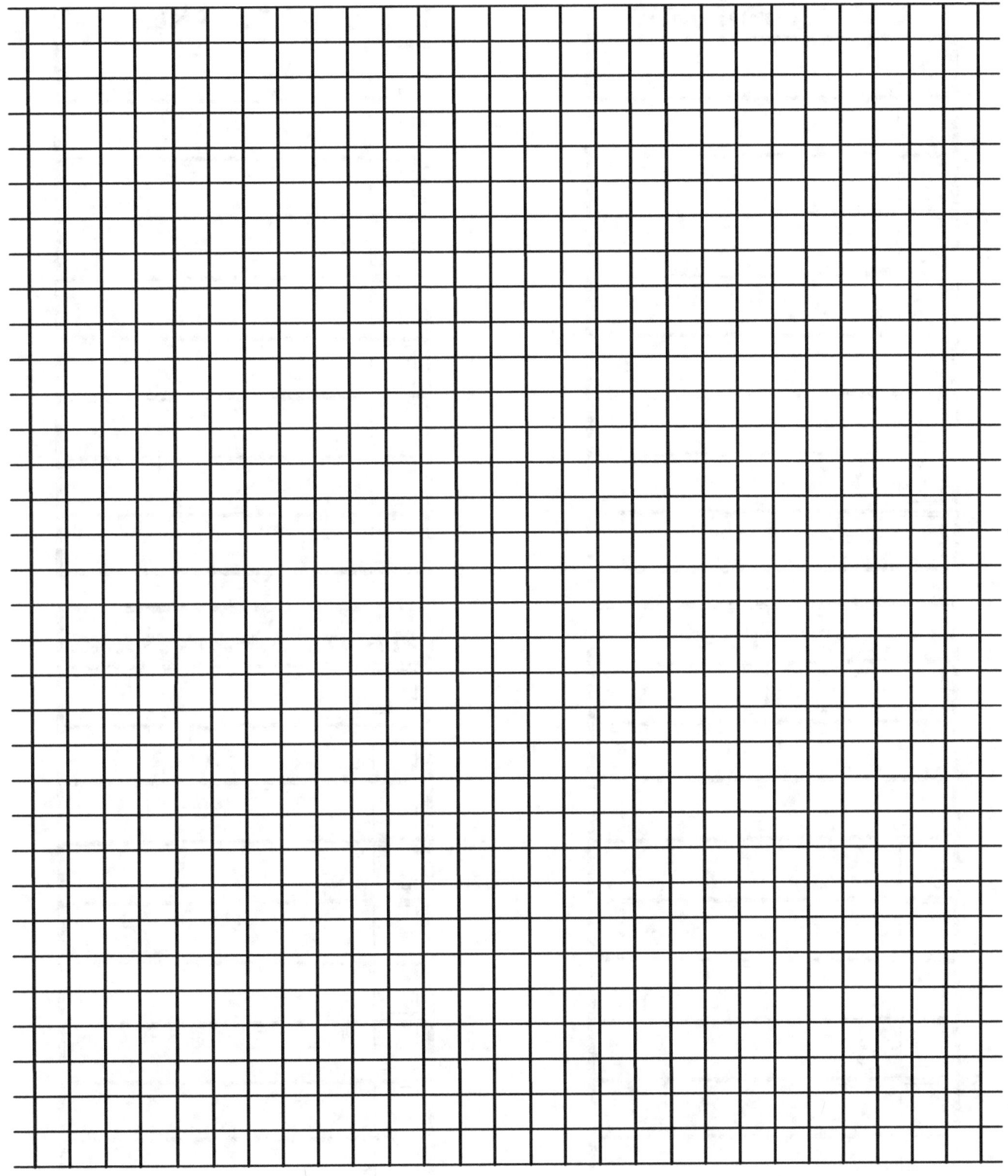

SEASONAL TASK

SEASON_____

GARDEN BEDS/ROW	MAINTENANCE

FERTILIZER	PLANTING/HARVESTING

Seed Inventory

CROP NAME	QTY	SOURCE	PURCHASE DATE	BUY MORE	YEAR
				Y/N	
				Y/N	
				Y/N	
				Y/N	
				Y/N	
				Y/N	
				Y/N	
				Y/N	
				Y/N	
				Y/N	
				Y/N	
				Y/N	
				Y/N	
				Y/N	
				Y/N	
				Y/N	
				Y/N	
				Y/N	
				Y/N	
				Y/N	

Seed Purchase

CROP VARIETY	QTY	COST	SOURCE	DISCOUNT

Seed Inventory

PLANT NAME	QTY	DESCRIPTION	WHERE TO BUY	WHEN TO BUY	
					☐
					☐
					☐
					☐
					☐
					☐
					☐
					☐
					☐
					☐
					☐
					☐
					☐
					☐
					☐
					☐
					☐
					☐
					☐

Plant Log

Crop Variety/Plant	Best Season to Plant	Plant Description	Additional Notes

Fertilizer Inventory

FERTILIZER	DESCRIPTION	PLANTS TO APPLY	QTY	BUY MORE	YEAR
				Y/N	
				Y/N	
				Y/N	
				Y/N	
				Y/N	
				Y/N	
				Y/N	
				Y/N	
				Y/N	
				Y/N	
				Y/N	
				Y/N	
				Y/N	
				Y/N	
				Y/N	
				Y/N	
				Y/N	
				Y/N	
				Y/N	
				Y/N	

Gardening Budget

ITEM	AMOUNT	AMOUNT SAVED

ITEM	AMOUNT	AMOUNT SAVED

ITEM	AMOUNT	AMOUNT SAVED

ITEM	AMOUNT	AMOUNT SAVED

Seed Starting Log

Crop/Seds	Date Planted	Date Germinated	Date Transplanted	Additional Notes

Expense Log

DATE	ITEM NAME	DESCRIPTION	QTY	COST	NOTES

SEASONAL CHECKLIST

SPRING

SUMMER

FALL

WINTER

PRODUCE BUDGET

FRUIT	VEGETABLES	WEIGHT	QTY	MONTHLY REVENUE	YEARLY REVENUE

Pest Control

Pest	Plants Affected	Bed/Raw	Problem	Tratament	Results

Monthly Garden Tasks

Top Priorities

_____
_____
_____
_____
_____
_____
_____
_____
_____
_____

To Do List

_____
_____
_____
_____
_____
_____
_____
_____
_____
_____
_____
_____

List of plants to try

_____
_____
_____
_____
_____
_____
_____
_____
_____
_____

Water

Sunlight

Fertilizer

Notes

_____
_____

Pest and Disease Control

Pest/Disease	Plants Affected	Bed/Raw	Problem	Tratament	Results

Monthly Garden Tasks

To Do List

Plant Name _____

Crop Variety _____

Fertilizer _____

Germination Date _____

Harvest Date _____

Seed Source _____

Plating instruction

_____
_____
_____
_____
_____
_____
_____
_____
_____

Water

Sunlight

Fertilizer

Notes

_____
_____
_____

Monthly To-Do List

Plant/Crop	Top Priorities	To-Do List

Monthly Garden Calendar
Month:_____

SUN	MON	TUE	WED	THU	FRD	SAT
☐	☐	☐	☐	☐	☐	☐
☐	☐	☐	☐	☐	☐	☐
☐	☐	☐	☐	☐	☐	☐
☐	☐	☐	☐	☐	☐	☐
☐	☐	☐	☐	☐	☐	☐
☐	☐	☐	☐	☐	☐	☐

Notes

Garden Layout

Garden Layout

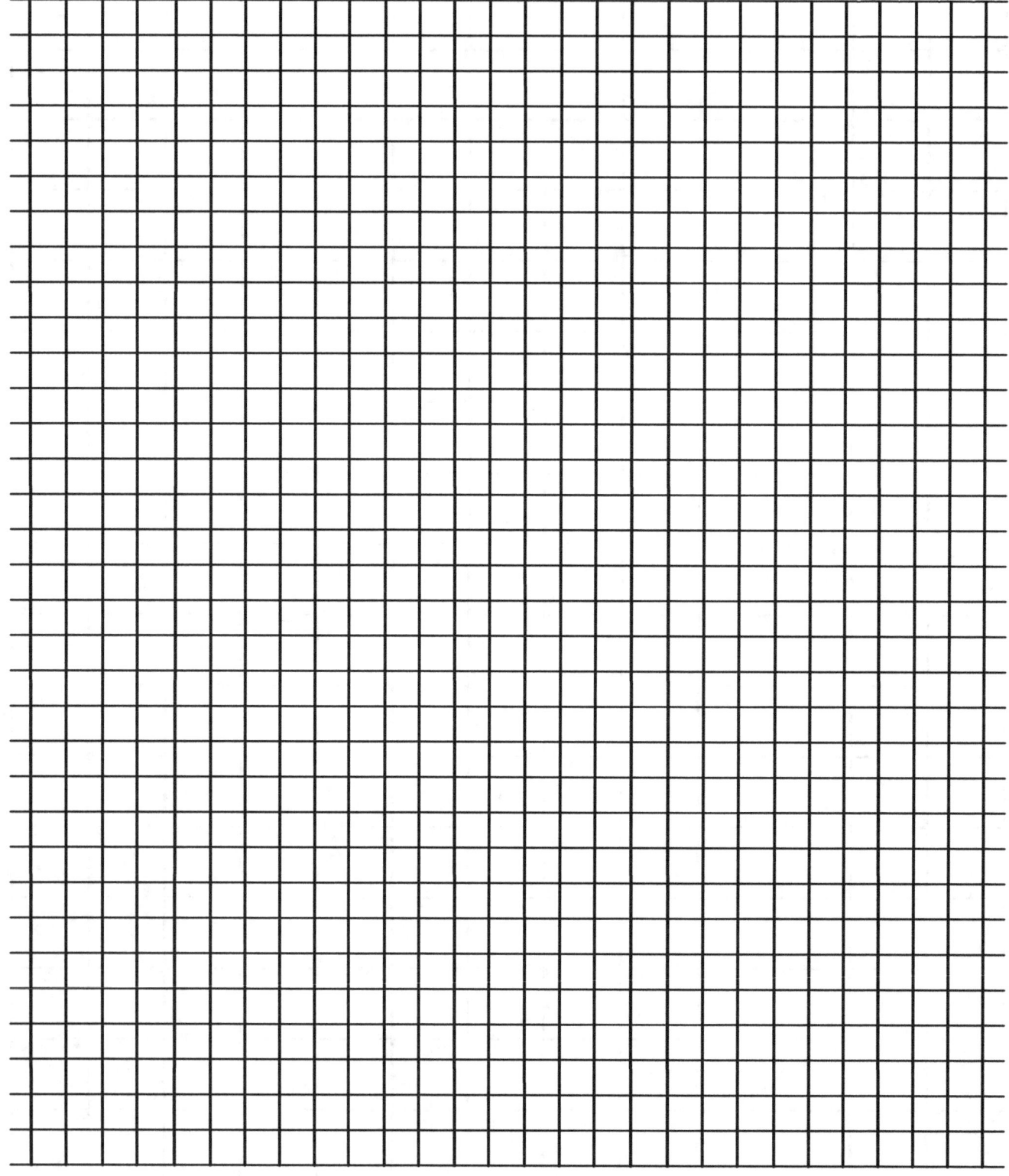

SEASONAL TASK

SEASON_____

GARDEN BEDS/ROW	MAINTENANCE
☐	☐
☐	☐
☐	☐
☐	☐
☐	☐
☐	☐
☐	☐
☐	☐
☐	☐

FERTILIZER	PLANTING/HARVESTING
☐	☐
☐	☐
☐	☐
☐	☐
☐	☐
☐	☐
☐	☐
☐	☐
☐	☐

Seed Inventory

CROP NAME	QTY	SOURCE	PURCHASE DATE	BUY MORE	YEAR
				Y/N	
				Y/N	
				Y/N	
				Y/N	
				Y/N	
				Y/N	
				Y/N	
				Y/N	
				Y/N	
				Y/N	
				Y/N	
				Y/N	
				Y/N	
				Y/N	
				Y/N	
				Y/N	
				Y/N	
				Y/N	
				Y/N	
				Y/N	

Seed Purchase

CROP VARIETY	QTY	COST	SOURCE	DISCOUNT

Seed Inventory

PLANT NAME	QTY	DESCRIPTION	WHERE TO BUY	WHEN TO BUY	
					☐
					☐
					☐
					☐
					☐
					☐
					☐
					☐
					☐
					☐
					☐
					☐
					☐
					☐
					☐
					☐
					☐
					☐
					☐
					☐

Plant Log

Crop Variety/Plant	Best Season to Plant	Plant Description	Additional Notes

Fertilizer Inventory

FERTILIZER	DESCRIPTION	PLANTS TO APPLY	QTY	BUY MORE	YEAR
				Y/N	
				Y/N	
				Y/N	
				Y/N	
				Y/N	
				Y/N	
				Y/N	
				Y/N	
				Y/N	
				Y/N	
				Y/N	
				Y/N	
				Y/N	
				Y/N	
				Y/N	
				Y/N	
				Y/N	
				Y/N	
				Y/N	
				Y/N	

Gardening Budget

ITEM	AMOUNT	AMOUNT SAVED

ITEM	AMOUNT	AMOUNT SAVED

ITEM	AMOUNT	AMOUNT SAVED

ITEM	AMOUNT	AMOUNT SAVED

Seed Starting Log

Crop/Seds	Date Planted	Date Germinated	Date Transplanted	Additional Notes

Expense Log

DATE	ITEM NAME	DESCRIPTION	QTY	COST	NOTES

SEASONAL CHECKLIST

SPRING

SUMMER

FALL

WINTER

PRODUCE BUDGET

FRUIT	VEGETABLES	WEIGHT	QTY	MONTHLY REVENUE	YEARLY REVENUE

Pest Control

Pest	Plants Affected	Bed/Raw	Problem	Tratament	Results

Monthly Garden Tasks

Top Priorities

_____
_____
_____
_____
_____
_____
_____
_____
_____

To Do List

_____
_____
_____
_____
_____
_____
_____
_____
_____
_____
_____
_____

List of plants to try

_____
_____
_____
_____
_____
_____
_____
_____
_____
_____

Water

Sunlight

Fertilizer

Notes

_____
_____

Pest and Disease Control

Pest/Disease	Plants Affected	Bed/Raw	Problem	Tratament	Results

Monthly To-Do List

Plant/Crop	Top Priorities	To-Do List

Monthly Garden Calendar
Month:_____

SUN	MON	TUE	WED	THU	FRD	SAT
☐	☐	☐	☐	☐	☐	☐
☐	☐	☐	☐	☐	☐	☐
☐	☐	☐	☐	☐	☐	☐
☐	☐	☐	☐	☐	☐	☐
☐	☐	☐	☐	☐	☐	☐
☐	☐	☐	☐	☐	☐	☐

Notes

Garden Layout

Garden Layout

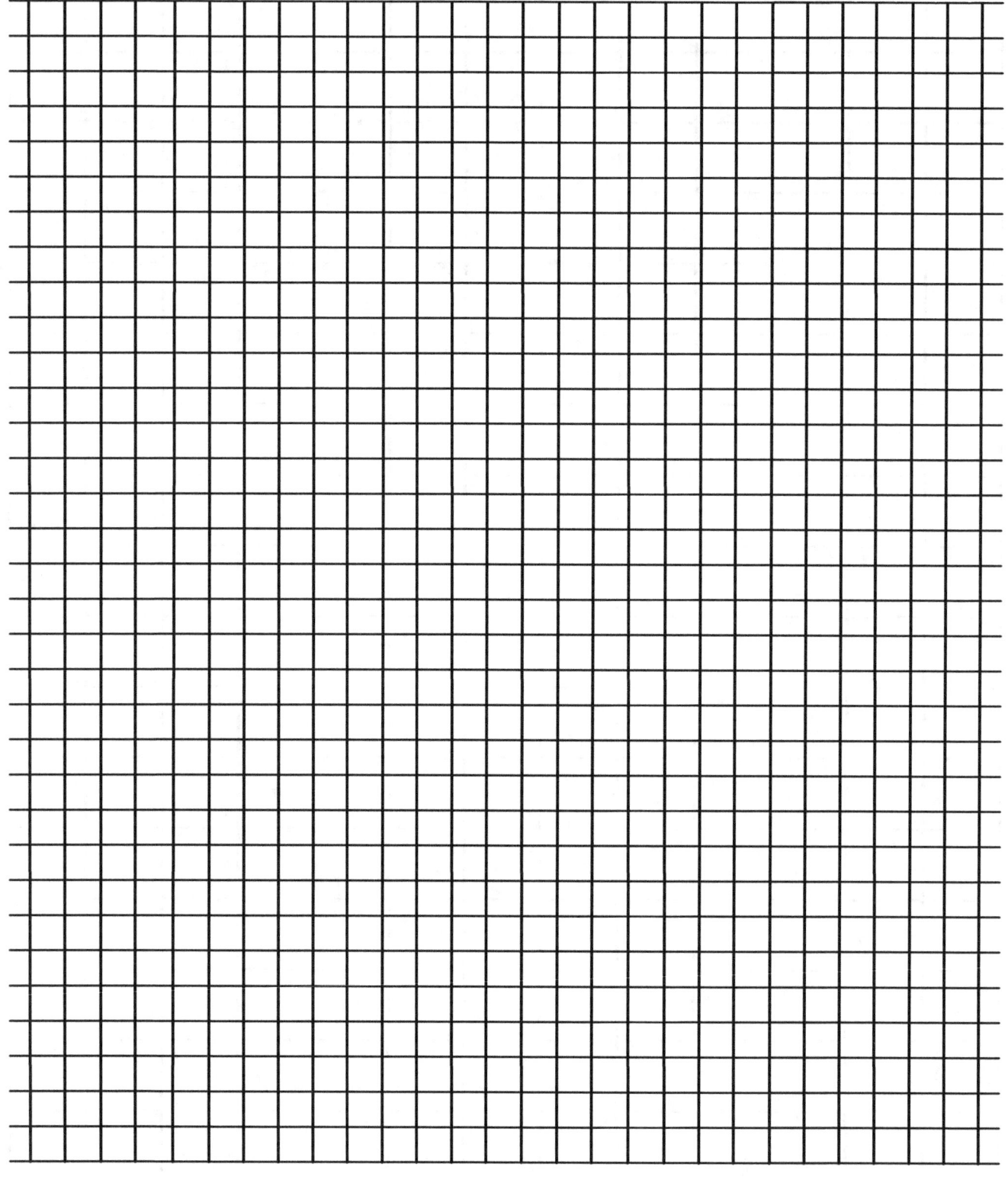

SEASONAL TASK

SEASON _____

GARDEN BEDS/ROW	MAINTENANCE
☐	☐
☐	☐
☐	☐
☐	☐
☐	☐
☐	☐
☐	☐
☐	☐
☐	☐

FERTILIZER	PLANTING/HARVESTING
☐	☐
☐	☐
☐	☐
☐	☐
☐	☐
☐	☐
☐	☐
☐	☐
☐	☐

Seed Inventory

CROP NAME	QTY	SOURCE	PURCHASE DATE	BUY MORE	YEAR
				Y/N	
				Y/N	
				Y/N	
				Y/N	
				Y/N	
				Y/N	
				Y/N	
				Y/N	
				Y/N	
				Y/N	
				Y/N	
				Y/N	
				Y/N	
				Y/N	
				Y/N	
				Y/N	
				Y/N	
				Y/N	
				Y/N	
				Y/N	

Seed Purchase

CROP VARIETY	QTY	COST	SOURCE	DISCOUNT

Seed Inventory

PLANT NAME	QTY	DESCRIPTION	WHERE TO BUY	WHEN TO BUY	
					☐
					☐
					☐
					☐
					☐
					☐
					☐
					☐
					☐
					☐
					☐
					☐
					☐
					☐
					☐
					☐
					☐
					☐
					☐
					☐
					☐

Plant Log

Crop Variety/Plant	Best Season to Plant	Plant Description	Additional Notes

Fertilizer Inventory

FERTILIZER	DESCRIPTION	PLANTS TO APPLY	QTY	BUY MORE	YEAR
				Y/N	
				Y/N	
				Y/N	
				Y/N	
				Y/N	
				Y/N	
				Y/N	
				Y/N	
				Y/N	
				Y/N	
				Y/N	
				Y/N	
				Y/N	
				Y/N	
				Y/N	
				Y/N	
				Y/N	
				Y/N	
				Y/N	
				Y/N	

Gardening Budget

ITEM	AMOUNT	AMOUNT SAVED

ITEM	AMOUNT	AMOUNT SAVED

ITEM	AMOUNT	AMOUNT SAVED

ITEM	AMOUNT	AMOUNT SAVED

Seed Starting Log

Crop/Seds	Date Planted	Date Germinated	Date Transplanted	Additional Notes

Expense Log

DATE	ITEM NAME	DESCRIPTION	QTY	COST	NOTES

SEASONAL CHECKLIST

SPRING

SUMMER

FALL

WINTER

PRODUCE BUDGET

FRUIT	VEGETABLES	WEIGHT	QTY	MONTHLY REVENUE	YEARLY REVENUE

Pest Control

Pest	Plants Affected	Bed/Raw	Problem	Tratament	Results

Monthly Garden Tasks

Top Priorities

To Do List

List of plants to try

Water

Sunlight

Fertilizer

Notes

Pest and Disease Control

Pest/ Disease	Plants Affected	Bed/Raw	Problem	Tratament	Results

Monthly To-Do List

Plant/Crop	Top Priorities	To-Do List

Monthly Garden Calendar
Month:_____

SUN	MON	TUE	WED	THU	FRD	SAT
☐	☐	☐	☐	☐	☐	☐
☐	☐	☐	☐	☐	☐	☐
☐	☐	☐	☐	☐	☐	☐
☐	☐	☐	☐	☐	☐	☐
☐	☐	☐	☐	☐	☐	☐
☐	☐	☐	☐	☐	☐	☐

Notes

Garden Layout

Garden Layout

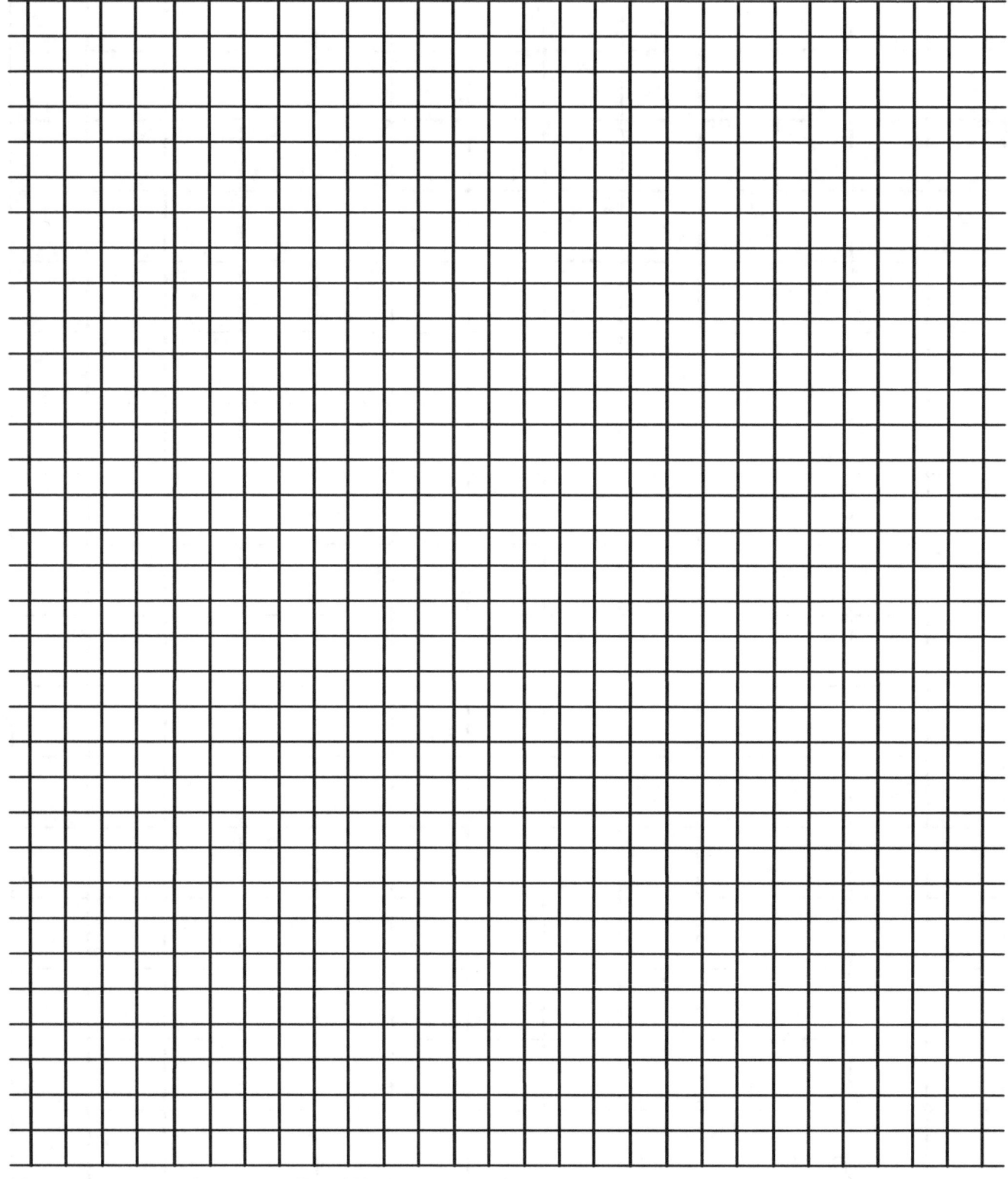

SEASONAL TASK

SEASON _____

GARDEN BEDS/ROW	MAINTENANCE
☐	☐
☐	☐
☐	☐
☐	☐
☐	☐
☐	☐
☐	☐
☐	☐
☐	☐

FERTILIZER	PLANTING/HARVESTING
☐	☐
☐	☐
☐	☐
☐	☐
☐	☐
☐	☐
☐	☐
☐	☐
☐	☐

Seed Inventory

CROP NAME	QTY	SOURCE	PURCHASE DATE	BUY MORE	YEAR
				Y/N	
				Y/N	
				Y/N	
				Y/N	
				Y/N	
				Y/N	
				Y/N	
				Y/N	
				Y/N	
				Y/N	
				Y/N	
				Y/N	
				Y/N	
				Y/N	
				Y/N	
				Y/N	
				Y/N	
				Y/N	
				Y/N	

Seed Purchase

CROP VARIETY	QTY	COST	SOURCE	DISCOUNT

Seed Inventory

PLANT NAME	QTY	DESCRIPTION	WHERE TO BUY	WHEN TO BUY	
					☐
					☐
					☐
					☐
					☐
					☐
					☐
					☐
					☐
					☐
					☐
					☐
					☐
					☐
					☐
					☐
					☐
					☐
					☐
					☐

Plant Log

Crop Variety/Plant	Best Season to Plant	Plant Description	Additional Notes

Fertilizer Inventory

FERTILIZER	DESCRIPTION	PLANTS TO APPLY	QTY	BUY MORE	YEAR
				Y/N	
				Y/N	
				Y/N	
				Y/N	
				Y/N	
				Y/N	
				Y/N	
				Y/N	
				Y/N	
				Y/N	
				Y/N	
				Y/N	
				Y/N	
				Y/N	
				Y/N	
				Y/N	
				Y/N	
				Y/N	
				Y/N	
				Y/N	

Gardening Budget

ITEM	AMOUNT	AMOUNT SAVED

ITEM	AMOUNT	AMOUNT SAVED

ITEM	AMOUNT	AMOUNT SAVED

ITEM	AMOUNT	AMOUNT SAVED

Seed Starting Log

Crop/Seds	Date Planted	Date Germinated	Date Transplanted	Additional Notes

Expense Log

DATE	ITEM NAME	DESCRIPTION	QTY	COST	NOTES

SEASONAL CHECKLIST

SPRING	SUMMER

FALL	WINTER

PRODUCE BUDGET

FRUIT	VEGETABLES	WEIGHT	QTY	MONTHLY REVENUE	YEARLY REVENUE

Pest Control

Pest	Plants Affected	Bed/Raw	Problem	Tratament	Results

Monthly Garden Tasks

Top Priorities

_____
_____
_____
_____
_____
_____
_____
_____
_____

To Do List

_____
_____
_____
_____
_____
_____
_____
_____
_____
_____
_____

List of plants to try

_____
_____
_____
_____
_____
_____
_____
_____
_____

Water

Sunlight

Fertilizer

Notes

_____
_____

Pest and Disease Control

Pest/Disease	Plants Affected	Bed/Raw	Problem	Tratament	Results

Monthly To-Do List

Plant/Crop	Top Priorities	To-Do List

Monthly Garden Calendar
Month:_____

SUN	MON	TUE	WED	THU	FRD	SAT
☐	☐	☐	☐	☐	☐	☐
☐	☐	☐	☐	☐	☐	☐
☐	☐	☐	☐	☐	☐	☐
☐	☐	☐	☐	☐	☐	☐
☐	☐	☐	☐	☐	☐	☐
☐	☐	☐	☐	☐	☐	☐

Notes

Garden Layout

Garden Layout

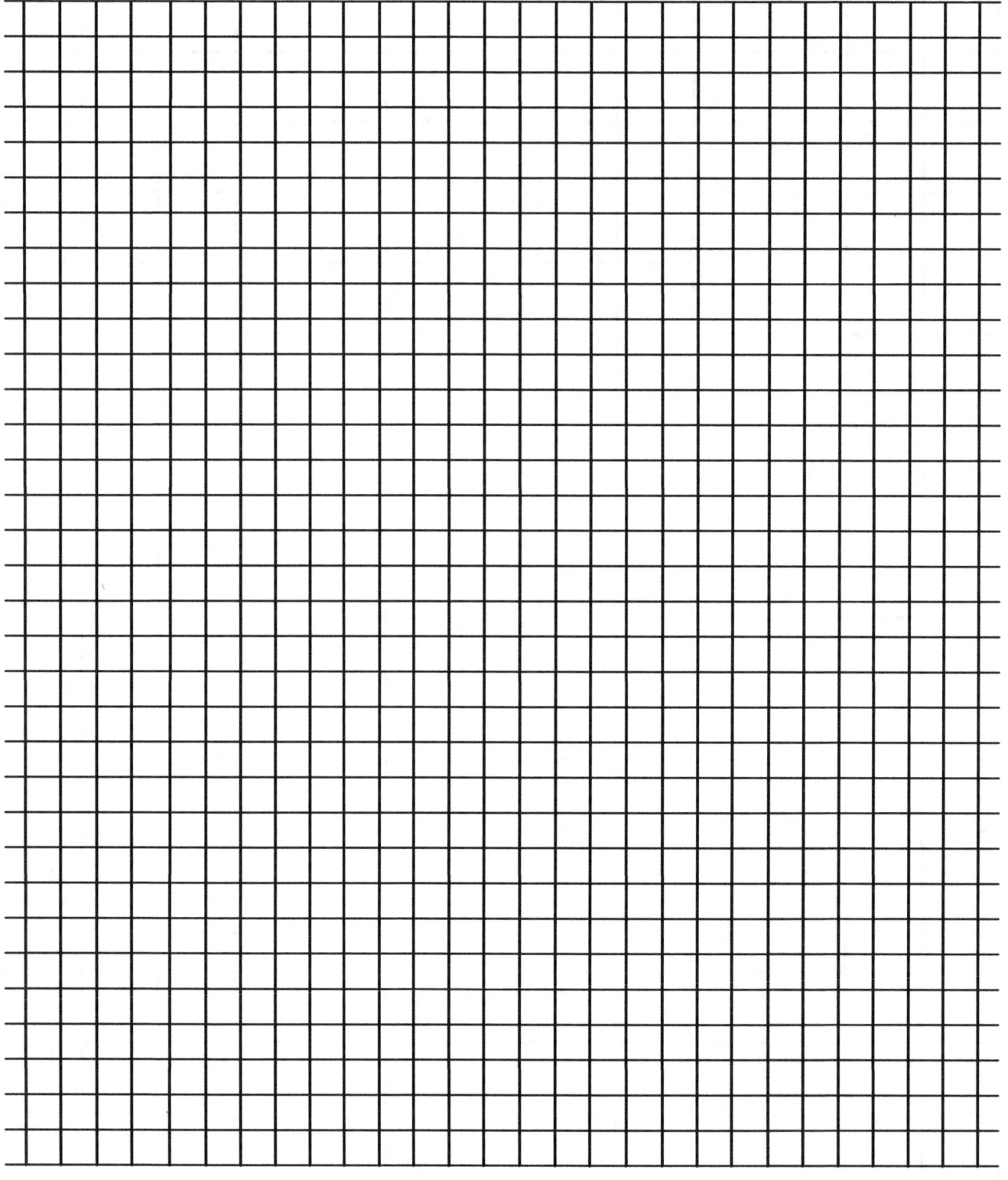

SEASONAL TASK

SEASON _____

GARDEN BEDS/ROW	MAINTENANCE
☐	☐
☐	☐
☐	☐
☐	☐
☐	☐
☐	☐
☐	☐
☐	☐
☐	☐

FERTILIZER	PLANTING/HARVESTING
☐	☐
☐	☐
☐	☐
☐	☐
☐	☐
☐	☐
☐	☐
☐	☐
☐	☐

Seed Inventory

CROP NAME	QTY	SOURCE	PURCHASE DATE	BUY MORE	YEAR
				Y/N	
				Y/N	
				Y/N	
				Y/N	
				Y/N	
				Y/N	
				Y/N	
				Y/N	
				Y/N	
				Y/N	
				Y/N	
				Y/N	
				Y/N	
				Y/N	
				Y/N	
				Y/N	
				Y/N	
				Y/N	

Seed Purchase

CROP VARIETY	QTY	COST	SOURCE	DISCOUNT

Seed Inventory

PLANT NAME	QTY	DESCRIPTION	WHERE TO BUY	WHEN TO BUY	
					☐
					☐
					☐
					☐
					☐
					☐
					☐
					☐
					☐
					☐
					☐
					☐
					☐
					☐
					☐
					☐
					☐
					☐
					☐
					☐
					☐

Plant Log

Crop Variety/Plant	Best Season to Plant	Plant Description	Additional Notes

Fertilizer Inventory

FERTILIZER	DESCRIPTION	PLANTS TO APPLY	QTY	BUY MORE	YEAR
				Y/N	
				Y/N	
				Y/N	
				Y/N	
				Y/N	
				Y/N	
				Y/N	
				Y/N	
				Y/N	
				Y/N	
				Y/N	
				Y/N	
				Y/N	
				Y/N	
				Y/N	
				Y/N	
				Y/N	
				Y/N	
				Y/N	
				Y/N	

Gardening Budget

ITEM	AMOUNT	AMOUNT SAVED

ITEM	AMOUNT	AMOUNT SAVED

ITEM	AMOUNT	AMOUNT SAVED

ITEM	AMOUNT	AMOUNT SAVED

Seed Starting Log

Crop/Seds	Date Planted	Date Germinated	Date Transplanted	Additional Notes

Expense Log

DATE	ITEM NAME	DESCRIPTION	QTY	COST	NOTES

SEASONAL CHECKLIST

SPRING

SUMMER

FALL

WINTER

PRODUCE BUDGET

FRUIT	VEGETABLES	WEIGHT	QTY	MONTHLY REVENUE	YEARLY REVENUE

Pest Control

Pest	Plants Affected	Bed/Raw	Problem	Tratament	Results

Monthly Garden Tasks

Top Priorities

_____
_____
_____
_____
_____
_____
_____
_____
_____

To Do List

_____
_____
_____
_____
_____
_____
_____
_____
_____
_____
_____
_____

List of plants to try

_____
_____
_____
_____
_____
_____
_____
_____
_____
_____

Water

Sunlight

Fertilizer

Notes

_____
_____

Pest and Disease Control

Pest/Disease	Plants Affected	Bed/Raw	Problem	Tratament	Results

Monthly To-Do List

Plant/Crop	Top Priorities	To-Do List

Monthly Garden Calendar
Month:_____

SUN	MON	TUE	WED	THU	FRD	SAT
☐	☐	☐	☐	☐	☐	☐
☐	☐	☐	☐	☐	☐	☐
☐	☐	☐	☐	☐	☐	☐
☐	☐	☐	☐	☐	☐	☐
☐	☐	☐	☐	☐	☐	☐
☐	☐	☐	☐	☐	☐	☐

Notes

Garden Layout

Notes

Thank you!

WE ARE GLAD THAT YOU PURCHASED OUR BOOK!
PLEASE LET US KNOW HOW WE CAN IMPROVE IT!
YOUR FEEDBACK IS ESSENTIAL TO US.

Contact us at:

 log'Sin@gmail.com

JUST TITLE THE EMAIL 'CREATIVE' AND WE WILL GIVE YOU SOME EXTRA SURPRISES!

www.ingramcontent.com/pod-product-compliance
Lightning Source LLC
Chambersburg PA
CBHW081623100526

44590CB00021B/3576